IMAGES
of America

TIVERTON
AND LITTLE COMPTON
VOLUME II

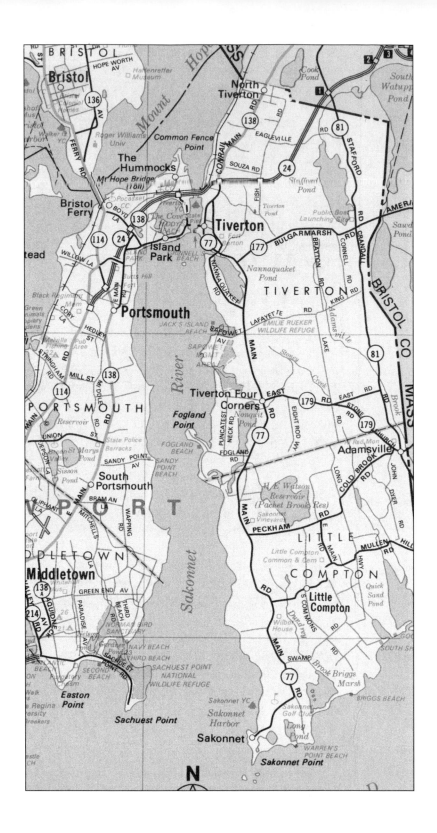

IMAGES
of America

TIVERTON
AND LITTLE COMPTON
VOLUME II

Nancy J. Devin and Richard V. Simpson

ARCADIA

First published 1998
Copyright © Nancy J. Devin
and Richard V. Simpson, 1998

ISBN 0-7524-1237-X

Published by Arcadia Publishing,
an imprint of the Chalford Publishing Corporation,
One Washington Center, Dover, New Hampshire 03820.
Printed in Great Britain

Library of Congress Catalog Card Number: 98-102729

Dedicated to the Wampanoag people of Pocasset and Sakonnet

Other publications by R.V. Simpson:
Crown of Gold: A History of the Italian-Roman Catholic Church in Bristol, RI (1967)
Independence Day: How the Day is Celebrated in Bristol, RI (1989)
Old St. Mary's: Mother Church in Bristol, RI (1994)
Bristol, RI: In the Mount Hope Lands of King Philip (1996)
Bristol, RI, Volume II: The Bristol Renaissance (1998)

Books by N.J. Devin and R.V. Simpson:
Portsmouth, RI: Pocasset: Ancestral Lands of the Narragansett (1997)
Tiverton and Little Compton, RI: Pocasset and Sakonnet, Wampanoag Country (1997)

Contents

This is an 1880 line representation of the Wampanoag Indians as they go about their daily pursuit.

Introduction

Tiverton

Native Americans gave the name Pocasset to the lands on both sides of the Seaconnet River. A portion of the first Tiverton settlement was known as the Pocasset Purchase. Initially, Aquidneck Island settlers grazed their animals at the southern portion of the town, at a place called Puncatest. Later, the land was settled through several individual purchases. The earliest land acquired, Nannaquaket Neck, was conveyed in 1651 through a private transaction between a white settler and the natives. (Please refer to Tiverton and Little Compton, Vol. 1 for information on the varied spellings of Nannaquaket.)

In 1674, John Simmons built a house and was licensed to keep a tavern. He also ran a ferry across the narrow passage between the Sakonnet and Mount Hope Bay. The Howland family ran the ferry c. 1700–1776, and thus the settlement on the Tiverton side of the Sakonnet assumed the name Howland's Ferry. The Howland name continued in use well into the 19th century.

After the death of King Philip on August 12, 1676, the remaining Wampanoag lands became open to white settlement. The Pocasset Purchase was made in 1680 by Plymouth Colony. In 1692 Tiverton became part of Massachusetts Bay Colony, and in 1694 it was incorporated as a township. Tiverton was annexed to Rhode Island in 1746. A portion of the original Pocasset Purchase land was given to Fall River in 1862 as part of the final settlement of a disputed boundary with Massachusetts.

During the Revolutionary War, a very important fortified redoubt called Fort Barton was occupied by a force of 10,000 armed Americans up on Tiverton Heights, overlooking Howland's Ferry. Although most residents approved of the war against the British, several remained loyal to the Crown. The most notable local Tory was Andrew Oliver, who had purchased Nannaquaket Neck around 1737. Oliver was Lieutenant Governor of Massachusetts. In 1775 the Colony of Rhode Island confiscated most of Oliver's land.

During the 19th century, Tiverton remained largely an agricultural community. Other enterprises included milling, textile manufacture, whaling, coastal trading, and fishing. Tiverton men played a premier role in the menhaden fish oil industry that prospered from about 1870 to 1910. When the railroad cut a path into the community, the town's recreational potential became a realization. In the late 19th century, two large cotton mills built at the northern border of town helped initiate the transformation of North Tiverton into an urban area.

At the dawn of the 20th century, the automobile put the entire town within easy reach of nearby urban centers. Particularly after World War II, this once-rural area became a residential suburb of Fall River. From the mid- to late 20th century, Tiverton Four Corners experienced a minor revitalization. Several century-old buildings were carefully restored. In what was formerly Pittsville, a metalworks was established in the 1960s on what had once been the site of a blacksmith shop, an icehouse, and a garage. The former gristmill and adjacent buildings were converted into offices and other commercial space.

Today the town is a multi-faceted community set within an essentially urban-suburban context. The legacy of the town's rich cultural resources is displayed in the historic landscape, structures, and villages from Stone Bridge to Bridgeport, and Fogland to Four Corners. A knowledge of these communities and their historic ties to Colonial days is important when trying to understand Tiverton's diverse heritage.

Little Compton

From its earliest history, the territory covered by Little Compton was inhabited by a sub-tribe of the Wampanoags called the Soughkonnet. At the time of settlement by English colonists the tribe was under the dominion of the Squaw Sachem Awashonks. From Awashonks, Constant Southworth and others received a deed on July 30, 1673, for a large portion of land in the westerly part of her territory. The first settlement in that area was made in 1674 by Captain Benjamin Church.

Contrary to mandates from Plymouth Colony, Little Compton did not immediately establish an official Congregational church. It was not until 1701 that a Congregational minister was in continuous residence in the town. By 1700, a sufficient number of Quakers, who had no interest in supporting a Congregational church, resided in the town and built their Quaker Meeting House. This mixing of Congregational and Quaker indicates a liberal attitude towards religious tolerance, which relates Little Compton more to nearby Rhode Island than to Plymouth Colony.

Politically, the town was equally independent-minded. At the end of the 17th century, during the time of war in Canada between England and France, Plymouth Colony increased the tax burden on its various towns to support the English cause. Little Compton, alone in Plymouth Colony, refused to pay until a military expedition marched into the town to enforce compliance.

The legacy of Little Compton's 17th-century development remains evident in the town's plan and network of roads. The plan is typical of townships established by Plymouth Plantation. The nucleus is the common land with meetinghouse, small house lots, and burial ground. Outlying lots are in larger parcels, originally ranging in size from 15 to 30 acres. The railroad never came to Little Compton—it is one of only four mainland Rhode Island towns that has never had rail service.

The economy of the town is modest and limited, with agriculture being its largest, and only, significant part. The Commons continues to serve as the focal point of the town, as it has since its founding. Indeed, it is unique in the state as a village that serves as an entire town's social and institutional focus while retaining much of its historical setting, buildings, and function.

Little Compton has an extraordinarily well-defined sense of "self," as well as a coherently built environment. Historically, it documents many phases of New England's rural, agricultural, and recreational past that have long since disappeared elsewhere. Above all, its historical legacy, a pre-eminent part of the town's collective consciousness, and its natural setting remain mutually balanced and enhanced.

Principle Reference Sources are: Providence Plantations for 250 Years (1886); Historic and Architectural Resources of Tiverton, Rhode Island: A Preliminary Report (1983); Historic and Architectural Resources of Little Compton, Rhode Island (1990); Little Compton Tercentennial (1675-1975); A Patchwork History of Tiverton, RI (1976).

One
Sakonnet River Bridges

Pictured here is the Tiverton approach to the Sakonnet River Railroad Bridge, *c.* 1906. The Fall River to Newport run of the Old Colony and Newport Railroad ran through some of the most scenic country in Bristol County. Over the years the line was operated by the New York, New Haven and Hartford Railroad, and later the Penn Central Railroad.

This is the Pocasset depot at the Portsmouth end of the railroad bridge, c. 1900. The trains served Aquidneck Island for over a century. Around the turn of the century, the train pulled some of the most luxurious cars in the world to Newport—private cars owned by the cream of Newport society.

Tiverton Station of the Old Colony and Newport Railroad is shown here, c. 1900. Stagecoach connections were made at this station for travelers going to Tiverton or Little Compton.

This photo was taken on September 21, 1938. In the aftermath of the surprise hurricane, Tiverton and Little Compton residents were shocked to discover both the railroad bridge and Stone Bridge washed away—they were completely cut off from the rest of Rhode Island.

Coastal defense was a concern in the early 1940s. A 20-inch coastal artillery gun is being unloaded from a railroad car. It will be trucked to the artillery battery at Seaconnet.

Flagman G.W. Russell checks at a crossing to make sure it's clear. The railroad served Aquidneck Island for over a century by way of the Sakonnet River Bridge. Trains functioned as a major transport vehicle for the island carrying passengers and freight for the local resorts.

Pictured here is engineer John Donahue. During the 1930s business slowed, but was revitalized during WW II when it served the Newport Naval Base with troops and supplies.

Conductor Russell Manning (left) and brakeman Archie Jordan prepare to begin the run to Tiverton from Newport in the fall of 1973. From the 1950s to the 1970s the trains hauled products that were too expensive to ship by other means: supplies for Kaiser aluminum, lumber and hardware for Weyerhaeuser and J.T. O'Connell, and unnamed cargoes for the Navy in Newport.

These are bridge gears that once turned the railroad swing bridge. Close inspection of the workings of the railroad swing bridge reveals remarkable engineering and construction. Fabricated in sections in Pennsylvania by the Pennsylvania Steel Company, the bridge was erected like a jigsaw puzzle. Much of the masonry was quarried from the nearby Hummocks in Portsmouth.

13

The train is passing through the railroad bridge approaching Tiverton Station, *c.* 1970. In the 19th century the railroads did just about whatever they wanted. Rather than build next to Stone Bridge in 1864, they located the first railroad bridge further north at the site of today's swing bridge. The gap was just as narrow as the Stone Bridge channel to the south, thus creating

a double bottle neck. A modified Baltimore through-truss span and a cantilevered assembly, about 220 feet long, compose the bridge's two identical trusses. The bridge's swing section is of tremendous weight—it rests atop an extraordinary center bearing made of phosphor-bronze, an extremely durable, low-friction material.

15

Train TX in Tiverton heads south on one of its last runs toward the Sakonnet River and Portsmouth.

Pictured is the Sakonnet River railroad swing bridge in closed position, *c.* 1954. In the foreground the new Sakonnet River Bridge is under construction.

Here is the Sakonnet River Railroad swing bridge as it appears today. The Sakonnet River Bridge, built at a cost of $9 million, opened with great fanfare on September 25, 1956, with Governor Dennis J. Roberts officiating.

This is an aerial view of the Sakonnet River Bridge, c. 1969. The replacement of the Stone Bridge simplified travel to Boston, Fall River, and Cape Cod from Aquidneck Island. The Portsmouth Town Council moved to demolish Stone Bridge in April of 1957.

Howland's Ferry at Stone Bridge is the subject of this photograph. In the foreground is the pedestrian's entrance to the toll bridge operated by the Rhode Island Bridge Company. The causeway and bridge at the narrows between Portsmouth and Tiverton have been an engineer's nightmare. In effect, the causeway acted as a dam against the incoming and ebbing tides.

Seen here is the old Stone Bridge from the Tiverton approach, *c.* 1907. Awaiting boaters approaching that narrow cut was a wall of roaring water. At the rate of 100 million gallons a minute, seawater churned through what was then a 33-foot-wide channel. It is said that the water was often a foot higher on one side of the bridge than the other.

This is the Rhode Island Stone Bridge as it appeared in 1907. The new, state-owned bridge featured a double-roller draw. Many a wrecked boat and several lost lives attest to the treacherous conditions. The channel's "hydraulic" problem attracted attention all the way to Washington, D.C., and even developed into a states' rights issue.

Stone Bridge looked like this after the 1938 hurricane. In the foreground is all that remains of Hopkin's Store.

GRINNELL'S GARAGE

Harry W. Grinnell

Proprietor

AUTOMOBILE REPAIRING, AUTO SUPPLIES
FISK TIRES, STANDARD GASOLINE
AND POLARINE OILS

Ford Car Agency

Automobiles for Rent by the Day or Hour

OPEN ALL NIGHT

MAIN ROAD

In the late 1800s the Stephen Grinnell family operated Grinnell's Stable located at the east boundary of Stone Bridge Inn on Lawton Avenue (then called Green Lane). In 1911 Harry W. Grinnell acquired the property and built Grinnell's Garage. This site is now occupied by the Getty gasoline station.

Two
Howland's Ferry Village and Stone Bridge Inn

Quite possibly the first ferry established in Rhode Island was licensed to Thomas Gorton in 1640. Operating in the vicinity of what was later Stone Bridge, it was first acquired by John Simmons and later, in 1694, by Daniel Howland. From 1694 until well into the 19th century, both the ferry and the immediately surrounding areas on the Tiverton side of the Sakonnet were known as Howland's Ferry. Daniel Howland, the innkeeper and proprietor of Howland's Ferry, was the son of Zoeth Howland of Dartmouth, who was murdered by Native Americans. Daniel was prominent in town affairs and for the first 20 years his residence was located near his ferry service. It was at his residence that the regularly scheduled town meeting assembled. Thus, the immediate area around the ferry grew to become Howland's Ferry Village, and eventually Stone Bridge Village.

This is the John Howland House, 1788 Main Road, *c.* mid-18th century. It was a gambrel-roofed cottage on the east side of the road at Stone Bridge. John eventually gave this house to his grandson John, who married Grace Church. It was later conveyed to a Mr. Hull and then sold to Aaron Baker. The first John mentioned was among the Tiverton incorporates in March of 1692.

Pictured here is Hambly's Blacksmith Shop, *c.* 1930. Early Tiverton land records refer to a Thomas Howland "who conveyed May 20, 1756 to Jonathan Devile (Davol), blacksmith, a certain piece of beach having a warehouse and the remains of an old wharf which was conveyed to said Howland virtue of a deed from ye proprietors of pocasset [*sic*] purchase."

This is Potter's Waiting Room, also known as Rounds's Waiting Room, c. 1910. This two-story, shingled building, academic in style, located in the vicinity of Lawton Avenue and Stone Bridge, was destroyed by the 1938 hurricane. The Stone Bridge commercial district extends south from South Avenue. It includes a group of buildings ranging in age from the mid-19th century to the late 20th century.

The original Lawton House was built around 1790 by Captain Lawton and was a well-known resort. Lawton House replaced the shanty inn of Howland's Ferry. It was built to provide "private and exclusive accommodations for those who may desire them." It was destroyed by fire in 1847. The second Lawton House, built in 1848 by Gardner Thomas, opened for business on July 4, 1848. It changed hands several times until being destroyed by fire in 1884.

Stone Bridge Cottage, 1800 Main Road, occupied a corner lot at the east end of what was once the Stone Bridge. Newport investor Asa T. Lawton bought the building in 1864, enlarging and generally improving it at the considerable sum of $60,000. The inn reopened in 1865 and operated for two seasons as Lawton House. In 1867, it was sold to a group of Fall River businessmen.

Stone Bridge Hotel is pictured here. The Fall River group operated the inn until the panic of 1878, when it was sold to Philander Smith. Smith ran the inn until selling it to Colonel George Alexander in 1884. On the exterior, the greatest change from the earlier building is the enclosure of the piazza that went around the building.

The Stone Bridge Hotel, shown here *c.* mid-1930s, was famous for its broiled live lobsters. Colonel Alexander had planned for a gala grand opening in June 1885, when the inn was again destroyed by fire. The Colonel then founded the Stone Bridge Hotel and Cottage Association and rebuilt the inn. The inn was renowned for its fine food and as a fashionable summer resort.

This is the view of the Sakonnet River from the Stone Bridge Hotel piazza. The inn changed hands several more times until the Feeney family bought it in 1921. The Feeneys and the Neys ran the inn successfully until 1965, when they retired from the business and sold it to Ralph Cutillo. Cutillo ran the inn, its restaurant, and banquet facilities until selling out in 1985.

This is the Stone Bridge Inn of November 1996. The new owner, James Pedro, ran the inn as a night spot, but sold out in 1987 to buyers who planned to build condominiums there. These owners went bankrupt, leaving the inn abandoned until Pedro bought it again in 1987. His plans to restore the inn never materialized.

The Stone Bridge Inn was demolished on Thursday, January 15, 1998. The last owner, Judith Roldan of Attleboro, wound up with the property after the previous owners defaulted on a loan she had made. Now an eyesore and a fire hazard, Roldan was under pressure from the town to raze the structure. (Photo courtesy of the January 22, 1998 issue of the *Sakonnet Times*.)

Three
Around the Sakonnet and Nanaquackett

This is a reenactment of the Battle of Rhode Island. Musket fire and black powder smoke fills the air during the annual reenactment. "Colonial" and "British" regiments from all over the northeast converge on Tiverton's Fort Barton area.

The Fall River (Tiverton) Yacht Club building is seen here after the 1938 hurricane. After the hurricane, the TYC used the present Standish Boat Yard building. In the 1950s the yacht club acquired its present quarters—the Bay View House.

Pictured here is the Tiverton Yacht Club on Riverside Drive. The clubhouse is sited on a small terrace above the road and near the water. The Bay View House was built in 1871 for use as a hotel by Philander Smith. In the 1890s it became a house of entertainment for transients, featuring weekly clambake dinners.

Pictured here is Almy's Wharf, or Fogland, c. 1912. Almy's Wharf off Fogland Road was a 240-foot-long structure with a 60-foot "T" at the end. It was built about 1903 at the south end of Fogland Beach. The *Queen City* and the *Islander* docked here on their daily runs between Sakonnet and Providence. The wharf was destroyed by fire in 1935, and was replaced by a short, 100-foot, stone wharf.

Coasters and fishermen are the subjects of this photograph. Small vessels, known as coasters, with shallow drafts able to negotiate shallow and restricted waters, plied Narragansett Bay and the Sakonnet River. Captain Peleg Cory of Tiverton ran a trading sloop from his wharf at Puncatest Neck to Providence with merchandise for Tiverton Four Corners in the early 19th century.

The Seaconnet Steamboat Company's *Islander* is pictured here. In 1886, Captain Horatio N. Wilcox opened a line between Sakonnet Point and Providence with a stop at Fogland using the steamer *Dolphin*. About one year later, Wilcox, with Captain Julius A. Pettey and others, organized the Seaconnet Steamboat Company. The run was made with the *Queen City* and the *Awashonks*. When the *Awashonks* burned in 1901, she was replaced by the *Islander*. This run continued until 1919.

Canoeing on the Sakonnet was popular in 1993. Art Waddicor (forward) and Jim Holland sail the Sakonnet, north of the railroad bridge.

This is the view from Upper Road (now Highland Road), *c.* 1900. This photograph and the two at the top of the following two pages form a panoramic view, south-to-north, of the Sakonnet River and general landscape in the Fort Barton area. The three panoramic photos were taken by Josephine Smithys, sister of Arvilla Meeson. (The reader should refer to Tiverton and Little Compton, Vol. I, pp. 21–23, for a five-photo panorama of the same area.) At this late date we can plainly see how sparsely inhabited the upper lands of the Stone Bridge, Fort Barton area were. Additionally, the simple, academic plan of the homes extant are a departure from the more elaborate architectural style of the 19th century. The most common type is the two-and-one-half-story, gable-roofed structure with a symmetrical five-bay facade, center entrance, and a large center chimney. Thirteen of Tiverton's early houses, however, are smaller, one-and-one-half-story cottages. Together the house and cottage form the basis of Rhode Island's domestic, vernacular architecture.

The Sakonnet, Spectacle Islands, and Blue Bill Cove are seen from the vantage point of Upper Road, *c.* 1900. These typical architectural forms remained an important part of Tiverton's building tradition and comprised a significant part of its houses well into the 19th century, largely defining the town's visual character. Depending on the age and scale of these early homes, they vary mostly in roof form, molding detail, and floor plan.

This is a similar view, taken *c.* 1907. This is an enlargement of a Dubois photograph. The principle structures have changed little, but the encroachment of newer structures is evident. Here we are afforded an excellent view of the Portsmouth Hummock.

Wide open spaces, the Sakonnet, and Stone Bridge are seen from Upper Road, *c.* 1900. Throughout rural Rhode Island in the 18th and 19th centuries, the five-room plan with center chimney remained the standard for both houses and cottages. The most unusual of Tiverton's early houses is the Job Gray House on Main Road. It is a one-and-one-half-story, three-bay facade, half-house—so-called because its chimney is located near one end. To the far right is Central Baptist Church, built in 1887.

This is the same general area as seen above, *c.* 1907. It is an enlargement of a Dubois photograph. Here we are afforded a view of the first Catholic church in Tiverton, St. Peter's by the Sea, and across the Sakonnet we have a view of the Church Brothers' Portsmouth fish processing plant.

Pictured here are Snell Bridge and Sin and Flesh Gut at high tide. Among the scenes of natural beauty within Tiverton, few surpass the attractiveness of Sin and Flesh Brook, which empties into Nannaquaket Pond at the Gut on Main Road. The brook was once dammed at several places to supply power to Tiverton's first yarn mill (destroyed c. 1864), gristmill, and sawmill.

The rugged beauty of Sin and Flesh Gut at low tide is captured here. The mill pond formed by the dammed brook supplied ice in winter. The brook also filled the pond of Sylvanus Nickerson, who operated a thread mill. Before Nickerson, the property was owned by brothers Moses and Aaron Baker—the brothers operated the grist and sawmills along the brook.

This is the Nannaquaket Bridge, before the 1938 hurricane. This view of the wooden bridge is from the Quacket River to Nannaquaket Pond beyond. The Bridgeport Market and fishermen's shanties can be seen on the left. In an act dated May 1875, the Rhode Island General Assembly authorized George W. Humphrey and others to erect a bridge across the strait leading into Nannaquaket Pond, providing, however, "that the said bridge shall be constructed at a place and upon a plan to be approved by the town council."

The contract for the construction was given to Charles E. Davis of Woods Hole and was signed July 5, 1883. Work began about August 1, and finished about November 1. The contracted cost of construction was $2,208, and the last 2 feet at the top of the structure were to be built by the owners, who evidently figured they could build this part cheaper using their own labor.

Davis agreed to pay for the rocks and stone delivered to the construction site by the owners. In the final settlement Davis allowed for 714 tons at 40¢ per ton. Furnishing this stone required a great deal of work by men and oxen, and incidentally resulted in the clearing of the fields and pastures of Nannaquaket.

Standing in splendid isolation is the Nannaquaket Neck home of Captain Nathaniel Boomer Church on the Quacket River. In building the causeway and bridge to his Nannaquaket Neck estate, Captain Church was the largest contributor.

Nannaquaket Bridge is shown after the 1938 hurricane. The stone and rubble-filled causeway is plainly seen. The stone masons and laborers engaged to finish the 1883 bridge, were compensated at the rate of 15¢ per hour. The sum of $420 was paid to Albert Gray and Thomas T. Gray for the south end of their wharf on the east side of the stream. At the time, there was an abandoned fish oil works on this property.

Pictured here is the tangled wreckage near Bridgeport Market after the 1954 hurricane. Eventually, the total cost of the original Nannaquaket Bridge exceeded $4,000.

Bruce Snell surveys the damage at Nannaquaket Bridge after the 1954 hurricane. The completed bridge was turned over to the town by its builders for public use. It was accepted by the town council in March 1884. Because of its solid construction, very little repair work has been required on the stone work, although the wooden span had to be replaced several times.

Pictured here is the stately, brick-gate entrance to Captain Church's Nannaquaket estate, *c.* 1907. The 1872 mansion is a large estate, conspicuously sited at the north end of Nannaquaket Neck, centered on a large, Second Empire house complex. When the estate was acquired by the Roman Catholic Diocese in the 1930s, holdings included a lot of approximately 20 acres, a 12-room house, a boathouse and pier, a large stable, and fruit and shade trees.

This is a view of Captain Church's Nannaquaket boathouse, *c.* 1910. Captain Church was master of several steamers, a menhaden agent in New York, and organizer of the American Fisheries Company. His wealth and influence made Nannaquaket a grand place. He retired in 1906.

The addition of open porches to the original 1870 building gave it a more horizontal and open look. The stable and carriage house, with quarters for a groom, is seen on the right. When the Captain gave his clambakes at the estate's boathouse for his Pogy boat skippers, his sister, Calista Church Cottrell, made gallons of her famous chowder.

Craftsmanship, restrained embellishment, and attention to detail is the hallmark of the N.B. Church house. Nannaquaket Neck began to develop in the 1950s. Land subdivision and the building of new homes went on at a lively pace. Today, the homes along Nannaquaket Road, on large lots, convey a quiet, pastoral, and pampered atmosphere.

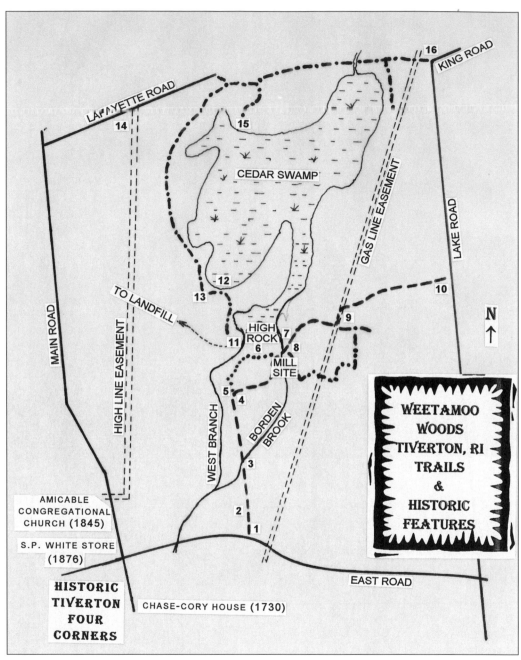

This is a detailed map of Weetamoo Woods. Legend: (1) Red trail, Eight Rod Way (Road), 1.5 miles to Lake Road; (2) Squire Chase Farm (private); (3) Borden Brook and slab bridge; (4) Mill Workers' Lot; (5) Beginning of Wordell Trail (skirts private property); (6) Base of High Rock; (7) Old Mill Site: 18th-century vertical sawmill stone remains, stone and earthen dike, and arched bridge; (8) Beginning of violet trail: loops through woods and rejoins red trail at (9) The walled-in farm site; (10) Lake Road; (11) Beginning of yellow trail, 1.5 miles to Lafayette Road, slab bridge; (12) Walled-in settlers' lot; (13) Giant oak tree; (14) Lafayette Road; (15) Wildcat Rock and hemlock forest; (16) parking, entrance/exit.

Four

Walk Weetamoo Woods

Welcome to Weetamoo Woods. This conservation area, named for the Squaw Sachem Weetamoo (which means Sweetheart), was dedicated May 20, 1990, and is owned by the Town of Tiverton. The area consists of 450 acres and is managed by the Open Space Commission, assisted by the Tiverton Garden Club's Open Space Committee. This public space is funded by the state and local open space bond program.

It is early spring in Weetamoo Woods. Conservationist and local historian Art Waddicor acts as tour guide. The first so-called slab bridge crossing Borden Brook is encountered on Eight Rod Way, about 100 yards from the park's south entry. This road was surveyed in 1679 as a proposed, but never completed, 132-foot-wide link between Sakonnet and Plymouth Colony.

The Red Trail begins on Eight Rod Way (Road). The "rod" is a British unit of measure. An 8-rod width was designated for this road so that 20 British soldiers could march in a line shoulder to shoulder. Art explained that the cobbles in the road were hauled from the beach and laid in inclines to give the oxen, used for hauling logs, improved footing.

This is the well-defined cellar hole of the home of mill worker Sippio (Scipion) Cook. Of particular interest is the garden, whose day-lilies along the south wall have become naturalized to the forest environment.

Pictured is the West Branch of Borden Brook. Here the brook runs wide and shallow with a network of fallen trees, limbs, and vines weaving a tangled highway used by forest creatures to traverse the morass. In the foreground is another slab bridge, one of several which the trails cross.

This view is north, as seen from the summit of High Rock. This rock out-cropping, and another called Wildcat Rock, are both 170 feet in elevation. In this view north, Art Waddicor adds scale to the vast Weetamoo landscape that is home to a half-dozen plants on the state's endangered species list.

Here is the path across the top of High Rock, looking south. The climb to the top of High Rock is short, but it can be strenuous. However, one is rewarded with a panoramic view of the park from above the forest canopy. Weetamoo's rock ledges, swamps, meadows, brooks, and old cellar holes provide habitats for several species of vascular plants, including mushrooms, lichens, and mosses.

Borden Brook, the remains of the Borden Sawmill, and a rare stone arch bridge are seen here. The 250-year-old stone arch bridge, the only one of its kind in the state of Rhode Island, was in immediate danger of collapse and was repaired in the summer of 1994. The project, under the direction of stone mason Brian Colvin of Scituate, took four weeks to complete and cost $9,000.

Pictured here is the completely restored arch bridge. Now, other than Brian Colvin and his assistant Albert Crowley (pictured), there is not a person alive who has experience in building a rock structure of this type. The bridge is held together by its own weight in an interlocking suspended arch. There is no mortar or tie of any kind.

Art Waddicor (middle left) adds scale to this picture of the view of the completed project from down stream. To rebuild the bridge the masons first braced it with a wooden frame. They maneuvered the rocks, some as heavy as 1 ton, by hand. No modern machinery was used in the reconstruction. The bridge is now 10 to 12 feet wider than before.

This is a view from above the arch bridge at the race-way. The site of the Borden Sawmill dates to the 18th century. The huge granite blocks used in the foundation as well as the stone remnants of the race-way and dam remain. The bridge was built to serve the sawmill. Reportedly, in the late 19th century, the mill was run by John Gray.

Five
Friendly Faces and Familiar Places

Charlie O'Brien, a landfill attendant, inspects one of the 40 stone markers in the pauper's graveyard south of the Tiverton landfill near the old Town Poor Farm (Asylum). The idea for a town farm for paupers was presented at an 1830 town meeting, and in 1831 the town bought a total of 60 acres from Edward Gray, Humphrey and Patience Gray, and the homestead of John Gray. The building was used as the town asylum until 1955 when it became a private rest home, operating until 1982.

This is the Brown, Reynolds, Meeson Homestead, also known as Lafayette House (1765, 1812), *c.* 1879, located at 3118 Main Road. It was a long, two-and-one-half-story home, with two interior brick chimneys, an asymmetrical six-bay facade with a small doorway right of center, and two entries at the rear. An ell, built by Abraham Brown, stood east of the main house. It was the original building, and was demolished in the 1940s.

Pictured here is the clapboard west front of Lafayette House in April 1998. The northern (left) part was built in 1765, and Isaac, Abraham's son, built the south portion in 1812. Later, a piazza was added across the front and left side. The piazza was severely damaged during the 1938 hurricane and subsequently removed.

This view shows the east and south sides (both shingled) of the Lafayette House. In the late 19th century, the place was purchased by Edward Meeson, a calico printer who had his business in Fall River. About 1928, Vincent Rose bought the place, and it is still owned by the Rose family.

This photograph is of the Lafayette House. At the rear is this four-bay carriage barn, a small shed, and a large, three-part barn or dairy with a stone-sided middle section. Nearby are the stone ruins (see above) of an old barn foundation.

Pictured from left to right are Frank Weeden, Tom Durfee, and John (Grampa) Reynolds, *c.* 1930. Grampa is Arvilla Reynolds Meeson's uncle. Because of the "Irish need not apply" mentality of the day, John was unable to find employment, so he opened his own fish market in Fall River.

The Old Stone Church (1841) and parsonage (1884) are pictured here. It is a simple, stuccoed, stone meetinghouse, set gable-end to the road, with a low, squat tower and a one-story addition at the rear. The plain facade has a pair of entrances placed at either side of the altar. The reason for placing the doors in this seemingly odd arrangement was so the faithful, while attending services, could also keep a watchful eye out for approaching danger.

It's clambake time at the Old Stone Church, c. 1914. Old habits and good bakes don't die easily. For almost a century, the last Saturday in July was the day of the annual clambake. Bakemaster Jimmy Roies, assisted by his wife, Lisa, prepare their bake in the traditional Rhode Island fashion. About 2:45 p.m. on bake day diners are invited to watch Jimmy and his helpers "pull the fire" and position the racks of food precisely over the red-hot stones and steaming ocean rock weed.

Seen here is the interior of the Nathaniel Briggs House, *c.* 1935. The portion of the house facing south is the oldest part. The northern service end was built to replace an earlier kitchen and service quarters, which were in an extreme state of disrepair due to long neglect. In the process of this replacement the original staircase was lost, as well as the large and spacious arrangement of the old kitchen—planned when slaves were available as family retainers. A new room was also added to the south front at its western end. This house is now one of the few remaining examples of the region's old manor houses. It reflects something of the vanished life and atmosphere of southern New England's old plantations. During the occupancy of Le Marquis de Lafayette at Abraham Brown's Main Road residence, Lafayette was entertained both formally and informally by Captain Briggs. (For more on the Briggs House see Tiverton and Little Compton, Vol. I.)

The Nathaniel Briggs, Manchester, Beattie House (pre-1777) is pictured here in April 1998. It is a very large, wood-shingled, colonial farmhouse with several large chimneys and two pediment entries on the east side. The structure includes a hip roof with small hip-roofed dormers. There is a large outbuilding with a fieldstone foundation at the rear of the lot, and a cemetery behind that.

This is the Nathaniel Briggs House south doorway, c. 1935. Captain Briggs, who built the house, was a slave trader—he reportedly kept slaves on the property. In the 19th century the house was owned by John Manchester (1790–1873) and his son Andrew. Andrew was a state senator and a state representative. For most of the 20th century the property was in the Beattie family.

This is the site of the original Gray's Ice Cream Parlor, also known as the Herbert Almy House, c. 1920. Mrs. Annie Gray sold ice cream out of the back window of this house from 1923 to 1937. All the cream was from local farms, but the ice cream itself was made in Fall River. Later, an addition was added onto the ice cream portion of the house which enabled Annie to make her ice cream in Tiverton.

Here is another view of Gray's original Ice Cream Parlor. Annie passed away in 1938, and her daughter, Florence Gray Brow, took over the ice cream parlor. Later, Florence sold the business to employees David Sylvia and Gilbert Pontes. In 1957 they tore down the old Almy House and constructed a new building. Sylvia and Pontes ran the business until 1979. In 1981 Marilyn Dennis took over the operation.

The 1957 Gray's Ice Cream Store is pictured here. This lot is where the original Almy House stood, and it is now Gray's parking lot. East Road passes in front of the building. The well-worn path leads to Main Road.

This photograph is of the Amicable Congregational Church (1845–1846 et seq), c. 1907. This edifice is a small but monumental Greek Revival building with a square, one-stage belfry and three stained-glass windows. The 1808 meetinghouse was destroyed by fire in 1845 and was immediately rebuilt according to plans submitted by Pardon Seabury. The large, polygonal bay, flanked by double-door entries, was added around the turn of the century.

55

Pictured here is Tiverton Town Hall (1825), *c.* 1928. On August 31, 1824, at a meeting of Freemen, Richard Durfee, Peter Estes, and Simeon Borden were appointed as a committee to report on the cost of building a town house. The following October they submitted a plan for a building 28 feet wide, 38 feet long, and 11 feet high. The estimated cost to build was $400.

These are the 1947 Ranger School graduates. Pictured from left to right are Barbara Oliveira, Barbara Davis, Jean Arruda, Jean St. Laurent, Beryl Riley, and Florence Carpenter.

The Riley Brothers' Store is pictured here in 1937. The Riley brothers, Raynor and T. Ashton, operated this small variety store and gasoline pumping station on Crandall Road. Helen Riley remembers the gas pumps dispensing Tidewater Gasoline at about 11¢ a gallon. As a general store, many hard-to-find sundries were carried. The store closed in 1972 and was reconfigured as a residence.

These are the children of Horace and Mina Almy, c. 1930. The family occupied the old Horace Almy Homestead on Punketest Neck Road. Known as "Nanquit Farm," the place was owned by Job Almy, then perhaps went to his son Otis, and in turn to his son Horace (1809–1874). The Almy's children, from left to right, are as follows: Laura, Clara, Nancy, Mabel, Ursilla, Louisa, Mina, Sidney, and Frederic.

This is a close-up view of the Town Whipping Post and sign on the John Almy House at Tiverton Four Corners. At one time, Tiverton Four Corners was Tiverton's "downtown." The major farm roads converged here, and it was the location of two general stores, the Red Store and the White Store. From approximately 1719 to 1812, on the land which is now Gray's parking lot, stood a lone, upright stone post. In 1794, the John Almy House was built on the same lot. The stone pillar was not moved, but rather preserved in its original location. To the early citizens of Tiverton, the post served a most practical purpose—it was the public whipping post.

Six

Little Compton and Adamsville

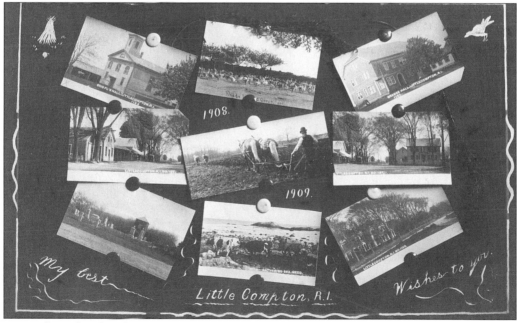

Generally isolated and remote, Little Compton is relatively free from the political pressures or economic forces that have transformed much of the rest of Rhode Island. The town's resistance to change (at first a result of its isolation, later due to deliberate decisions) has preserved a remarkable legacy that presents an idyllic picture—with rolling topography, stout stone-wall-bounded farms, woodlands, marshes, saltwater ponds, barrier beaches, the rocky cliffs of Sakonnet Point, old farm homesteads, fashionable summer retreats of wealthy city dwellers, and tree-lined winding roads. In this section, the reader is transported by way of an imaginary carriage ride along dusty, turn-of-the-century roads, from Adamsville to Sakonnet Point.

LET · SE · NOW · WHO · SCHAL TELL FIRST A TALE

This is the sitting room of the Elizabeth Alden Peabody House, c. 1910. This house is popularly associated with the daughter (1623–1717) of John Alden and Priscilla Mullins. The attribution is due to the 17th-century appearance of the homestead as well as the possibility that Elizabeth lived here with her son after her spouse died in 1707. Elizabeth's grandson John (1700–1767) sold the house to Pardon Gray (1737–1814) in 1762, and the Grays soon added the portion of the house west of the front door. (See Tiverton and Little Compton, Vol. I, pp. 85–87.) The two-story bay window on the west side, designed by Little Compton artist Sydney Burleigh, was added at the end of the 19th century.

Spite Tower is shown here on Westport Harbor (South) Road, c. 1910. Adamsville is one of those places the tourist guides like to describe as "off the beaten path." It is refreshingly quiet— a Sunday-sort-of-place. Seemingly contradictory to being a small rural town, Adamsville has a building that can claim "skyscraper" status: Spite Tower. The story behind the 45-foot tower is an intriguing one, owing something to both fact and legend. Around 1905, Abraham Manchester took over, from his father, management of his Adamsville store. His sisters, Deborah and Elizabeth, lived in the family home across the street, but Abraham lived above the store. When he wished to send a simple message to his sisters, he did so by waving a cloth out the store's second-floor window.

Here is Abraham Manchester's store, c. 1820. The system Manchester had with his sisters worked well until Dr. John Hathaway took residence with his wife, Claudia, on the property between the store and the Manchester home. Local legend suggests the doctor had a romantic interest in one of the Manchester sisters. It is doubtful if Spite Tower was built at the time this early postcard was published.

A closer view of Manchester's store is had here, c. 1905. When the doctor's love interest received no response, he had the tower built at just the right point to block the formerly unobstructed view between Abraham and his sisters, thus frustrating communication from one to the other. (For more on the Manchesters and Spite Tower see Tiverton and Little Compton, Vol. I, p. 64 and 71.)

Visible here is the Adamsville access to the Acoaxet River, c. 1910. Nestled in a valley at the convergence of several roads and at the head of the Acoaxet River, Adamsville spreads across two towns: Little Compton, RI, and Westport, MA.

The dirt Harbor Road is pictured here, c. 1905. Local tradition maintains that Adamsville was a minor port and maintained a snug harbor in the 18th and early 19th centuries. This is documented by the Blaskowitz map of 1777, which shows the Acoaxet River navigable to Adamsville.

Pictured here is the village stable and smithy, c. 1905. In rural New England towns and villages, the local smithy was indispensable. Besides shoeing horses and oxen, he was the maker and mender of tools for home and farm. (Photo courtesy of Millicent A. Waite.)

Seen here is (West) Main Street, Adamsville, c. 1910. The authors located this spot with little difficulty. Although much has changed, much has remained the same. The elm trees and the cottage on the right are no longer in existence. However, the utility pole and stone wall (left) are still there. The gap in the stone wall (right) where the cottage porch is seen is now blocked with stones of the same kind, and a grassy field has replaced the cottage. The shuttered windows (right) belong to the Electra Lodge Number 41, Independent Order of Odd Fellows (c. 1877–1878). This building is now the home of Stonebridge Dishes.

Gray's Cash Store (1788) and Little Compton's first post office (1804) are the subjects of this c. 1905 photograph. By 1820, the village had at least one general store, operated by Ebenezer P. Church. In the middle of the 19th century, Adamsville counted some 20 houses, a sawmill, a carding mill, a gristmill, a post office, a smithy, and two stores—Gray's and Manchester's. (Photo courtesy of Millicent A. Waite.)

This is the lane to Joshua Bailey Richmond's country seat, 59 South of Commons Road, *c.* 1905. J.B. Richmond (1843–1931) acquired his father Isaac's (1798–1888) estate upon his death. The farm, including a large, rambling, clapboard house, faces south across rolling, open fields. The Richmond house is set within a well-landscaped setting surrounded by extensive gardens, shade trees, winding drives, and several handsome outbuildings. Joshua worked as an importer, manufacturer, and sugar refiner who lived on Boston's posh Beacon Street. He retired in 1890 and soon after, began transforming his father's working farm into a handsome country estate. During the first decade of the 1900s, Joshua began acquiring land around the family homestead and his children built their vacation houses on these parcels.

Seven

Around the Commons

As a remote town, with only negligible industrial potential, Little Compton developed only two real villages—the Commons and Adamsville. A third settlement, now gone, existed at Sakonnet Point. The 17th-century Commons was centrally located and has remained the pre-eminent village within the town since its creation. Its civic role was intensified as new buildings were erected around its periphery through the 19th century. The meetinghouse and the Congregational church were supplemented by the Methodist church (see Tiverton and Little Compton, pp. 74–75), stores, blacksmith's forge, and civic buildings.

Pictured here is the Odd Fellows Hall, a Greek Revival temple in the American vernacular, *c.* 1905. The public architecture of Little Compton is simple. Like that of most rural New England towns, it is rooted in local traditions, yet it participated in trends in American architecture. During the 1830s and 1840s, Little Compton participated in the national direction in civic and public building (the Greek Revival style).

This is a photograph of the Number 8 Schoolhouse, *c.* 1845. The form of this building is similar to that used throughout the state for one-room schoolhouses at the time. The building continued to function as a school until the completion of the Wilbour School in 1929.

This is a drawing of Little Compton's first town hall. The original town house, which served both religious and civic gatherings, was built on the Commons in 1693. This building stood until 1917, when it was destroyed by fire.

The interior of the first town hall is shown here. This is an old drawing used by Isaac C. Wilbour in a magazine article c. 1882. It is incorrect, for it depicts a brick or stone construction, when the building is of a wood-frame construction. It shows four windows where there should be three. However, the general representation is correct, especially as to the gallery, desk, benches, and inclined planks used to ascend to the seating places.

Pictured here is Wilbur's Store in the early to mid-19th century. Arthur "Pop" Wilbur stands beside his brand-new Model A Ford in front of his store at 2 South of Commons Road. It was a small one-and-one-half-story, clapboard building, set gable-end to the street, with a center entrance flanked by plate-glass windows and two symmetrically placed, two-over-two, sash windows in the attic. A large, rectangular sign reads, "Est. of C.R. Wilbour General Merchandise."

Pictured from left to right, Arthur Wilbur, Otho Wordell, Ida Wilbur, Leonard Sylvia, Clarence Kelly, and Harold Brownell pose in front of Pop Wilbur's store. A general store has been at this location since the early 19th century. Located at the eastern edge of the Commons, Wilbur's Store is a town institution and meeting place. It was heavily damaged by fire in 1980, but was immediately rebuilt and appears much as it always has.

The old Methodist Meeting House (1825) is seen here, *c.* 1935. It was a shingled, two-and-one-half-story house, with paired interior chimneys, and a five-bay facade and center entrance within a one-story porch. The rear portion of this building originally served as the Methodist church on West Main Road. It was moved to the Commons in 1839, and the front portion was built the following year.

This is the Oliver C. Brownell House (*c.* 1850), *c.* 1900. The Brownell House was a handsome, two-and-one-half-story clapboard dwelling with paired interior chimneys and a one-and-one-half-story ell parallel to the main portion at its southeast. The main block has a three-bay facade and center entrance within a one-story, bracketed porch with palmette-and-anthemion iron cresting. Above the porch is a pair of round-head windows. The addition of the fine, cast-iron fence, also with palmette-and-anthemion detail, adds to the elegance of this well-cared-for residence.

The Brownell-Bodington House is the subject of this *c.* 1905 photograph. The Bodingtons bought the Brownell house and barn for $5,500. Although always a residence, for a while it was Little Compton's post office, with Gram and Granddad Bodington serving as postmasters. Townfolk wishing to post mail slipped it through the mail slot in the door on the south side of the house by the piazza. You can still see the mail slot, but it has since been sealed.

Pictured here is a handsome and rugged stone-and-timber outbuilding. Such finely constructed buildings are typical of those found on several of Little Compton's former working farms and country seats.

Here is one of the many farm lanes that crisscross Main Road, c. 1900.

It was a busy day on the Commons around the Brownell House (1850), *c.* 1890. The gentleman carrying the small satchel may be a physician, and we can assume the nearby, unattended carriage is his conveyance. Note the slender circumference of the elm trees in this photograph as compared to their later, healthy girths in the previous snapshot. This property was later purchased by Frederick A.H. Bodington, who came to America from England at age seven. He bought the house in the late 1800s. A hard-working individual, invested with the American dream, he employed himself at many jobs: he raised geese and drove them on foot to Boston for sale, he owned or managed an ice business and wood lots, he gave horseback-riding instructions,

and he skippered a Sakonnet steamer. Eventually, Frederick became The Honorable Senator Bodington, a member of the Rhode Island General Assembly.

Today the Commons continues to serve the town as it has through its recorded history. With a school, church, town hall, post office, restaurant, stores, and offices (some of them occupying structures erected as dwellings), it is very much the town's gathering place. Indeed, the Commons is unique in the state as a village that both serves as a whole town's social and institutional focus while retaining much of its historic setting, buildings, and functions.

The Congregational Parsonage (1870) is seen here, c. 1910. It is a two-and-one-half-story dwelling, with a three-bay facade, center entrance, bracketed hoods over doors and windows, and bracket-and-dentil cornice. This parsonage was built for the nearby Congregational church just before the church itself was considerably remodeled.

This picture was taken in the Old Burying Ground (1675 et seq.). The stone markers of (left) "Elizabeth, who should have been the wife of Simeon Palmer . . ." and (right) ". . . Lidia ye wife of Mr. Simeon Palmer . . ." are among the neat, north-south rows of tombstones, the earliest of which date from the 17th century.

These are the graves of Captain Benjamin Church and Alice Southworth, his wife. Church is widely acclaimed as the ". . . vanquisher of King Philip." King Philip's War brought to a bloody climax more than 50 years of English-Native American relations in New England and eliminated the Native Americans as a major factor in the southern New England settlements. One cannot read of the encroachment of the settlers upon the native population and the whittling away of their lands, dignity, and independence, without a genuine sense of remorse.

Pictured here is Captain Benjamin Church (1639–1718). Church adopted Native-American-style tactics to defeat Metacomet's warriors in King Philip's War. This questionable likeness was engraved by Paul Revere to accompany the publication of Church's account of his actions that brought defeat to the Wampanoags.

[The following is an exact copy of the title page of the old edition.]

THE

ENTERTAINING

HISTORY

OF

KING PHILIP'S WAR,

WHICH BEGAN IN THE MONTH OF JUNE, 1675.

AS ALSO OF

EXPEDITIONS

MORE LATELY MADE

AGAINST THE COMMON ENEMY, AND INDIAN REBELS, IN THE
EASTERN PARTS OF NEW-ENGLAND:

WITH SOME ACCOUNT OF THE DIVINE PROVIDENCE
TOWARDS

COL. BENJAMIN CHURCH:

BY THOMAS CHURCH, ESQ. HIS SON.

SECOND EDITION.

BOSTON : PRINTED, 1716.

NEWPORT, RHODE-ISLAND : REPRINTED AND SOLD BY
SOLOMON SOUTHWICK, IN QUEEN-STREET, 1772.

This is the title page of the *History of King Philip's War*, which was written by Colonel Benjamin Church.

The monument to Elizabeth Alden Pabodie (Peabody) is shown here. Elizabeth was the daughter of Plymouth pilgrims John Alden and Priscilla Mullin, and the first white female born in New England. She was the spouse of William Pabodie. She died on May 31, 1717, in her 94th year.

George S. Burleigh, beloved Little Compton poet, is the subject of this *c.* 1900 photograph. Mr. Burleigh's literary labors were largely devoted to magazine productions and editorial work. Publications for which he won renown are: *Anti-slavery Hymns*, 1842; *The Maniac and Other Poems*, 1849; *Signal Fires*, 1856; and a translation into English verse of Victor Hugo's *La Legende des Siecles*, 1867. It is he who composed the verse engraved on the Elizabeth Alden monument.

Pictured here is the old town house, *c.* early 1890s. The town's first town house served both civic and religious gatherings. Located on the Commons in back of the "White Church," this was for many years the site of the Commons branch of the post office. (See page 69.)

One-stop shopping was possible in this area, c. 1915. The post office and barber shop were on the ground floor, and the telephone exchange and Allen's Shoe Repair and Harness Shop were on the second floor. The foul breath of exhaust fumes had yet to pollute the air of the Commons. Spring and the scent of primrose in the clean country air were joys soon to pass with the arrival of the motorcar.

Here is a picture on the Main Road, c. 1905. There was plenty of dust around in those days. Passing wagons and pawing hooves sent up clouds of dust, and the southwest breezes distributed dirt impartially and in abundance.

Renovation of the United Congregational Church tower was done in May of 1974. This photo was taken in April as the steeple was removed to facilitate repairs to rotted underpinning in the ancient edifice. The modern, Gothic detail on the tower and spire date from 1871. The tower serves as a town landmark and is visible from many parts of the surrounding area.

Eight
Nineteenth-Century Little Compton:
A Traveler's Guide

This is a painting of a Little Compton hay field by Sydney R. Burleigh, c. 1905. Burleigh lived and worked in Providence for most of his career, but he maintained a home and studio on the Sakonnet shore in Little Compton. Little Compton, with its rural purity and working farms, became Burleigh's favorite subject matter after about 1890. The artist's talent took many forms, including designing, carving and painting furniture, making jewelry, and designing interiors. However, he is best remembered for his watercolor depiction of rural scenes that he exhibited annually at the Providence Art Club and the Providence Water Color Club.

Awashonks Stone is shown here, *c.* 1915. Occasionally, 19th-century historians failed to record happenings and sites that seemed at the time to be insignificant. Such is the case with the two photographs presented on this page. During the first two decades of this century, itinerant photographers traveled the highways and back roads of America to record beauty and curiosity. The only large stone in Little Compton of historic importance known to the authors is Treaty Rock. This so-called Awashonks Stone may be her "throne," similar to King Philip's Throne on Mount Hope in Bristol.

Here we are, hearth-side at Brimstonehill Farm, an unknown farm in Little Compton, *c.* 1915. The Federal-style mantle dates this room to the period when this style was popular (early- to second-decade-1800s). The reader is encouraged to view this photograph with a strong magnifying glass—it is full of interesting early-19th-century details.

The Wilbour House (c. 1690), located at 548 West Main Road, is now the site of the Little Compton Historical Society headquarters. It is a two-and-one-half-story, weathered, clapboard-and-shingle house with a large center chimney and ell at the rear. The center entrance in the asymmetrical four-bay facade has a transom light. The windows in the eastern half of the house are considerably smaller than those on the west. The historical society acquired the house in 1955 and undertook its careful restoration as a museum.

Shown here is the interior of Sidney R. Burleigh's studio, "Peggotty," (c. 1906). Sheltered by a lean-to on the grounds of Wilbour House is the former catboat-turned-artist's studio. Burleigh hauled the abandoned ferry to his garden, where he built a superstructure and furnished it as seen here.

The Stewart Carton Farm gate is pictured here. Little Compton's long agricultural development has shaped the landscape of the town. The creation of stone-walled fields, the establishment of a network of paths, lanes, and roads among these fields, and the buildings in farm complexes have created an extremely picturesque rural setting recalling the farming that occurred here over several centuries.

Toward the end of the 19th century, except for horses and cows, the livestock population declined. Between 1885 and 1895, butter production declined considerably, while milk production increased dramatically from 23,049 gallons to over 213,000 gallons, and egg production increased from 106,500 to nearly 3.5 million. This is probably due to the opening of markets in Providence, Fall River, and Boston.

This is the B.F. Wilbour Place. The authors are unsure of the exact location of this homestead. We are sure the initial "F" is for Franklin, but no structure owned or built by Franklin Wilbour is listed in our principle source, *Historic and Architectural Resources of Little Compton*. A Bennet Wilbour House is listed at 11 Shaw Road, but the description of the Shaw Road property does not fit the building pictured here.

Pictured here is "Seaconnet House," or the Richmond House (*c.* 1850). As early as the 1850s it functioned as a country inn. Two large wings in the rear, now removed, accommodated guests. Isaac B. Richmond operated this hotel in the 19th century, and his heirs continued to own the property until the 1970s. Before the founding of the Sakonnet Golf Club in 1909, summer residents used the acreage around this house as golf links.

This is Main Road at the corner of Seapowet Road. Small lanes and paths that edged the fields or passed between them connected the farmland with the farmhouse and its outbuildings. Now diminished as agricultural pursuits have become less pervasive, networks of lanes and paths survive both as farm lanes and private roads to houses or residential complexes.

The Edward D. Duffield House (*c.* 1906), located at 26 Atlantic Avenue, is shown in this *c.* 1915 photograph. Elizabeth Curtis Duffield first came to Little Compton in the summers to visit the Aldens. She built this house around the time of her marriage to Edward. The Duffields lived in South Orange, New Jersey.

Shown here is the Colonel Amasa Gray House (*c.* 1685), 361 West Main Road, *c.* 1915. The earliest part of this house is almost completely engulfed by many additions. The northern section was destroyed by fire in 1984.

The Church-Burchard Residence, or "Old Acre" (*c.* 1841), located at 420 West Main Road, is the subject of this *c.* 1915 photograph. This estate is one of the finest Colonial Revival country seats in the state. John Church (1794–1882) was a successful Providence architect and builder. He retired to Little Compton in 1840 and built this house shortly thereafter. Roswell Burchard (1860–1931) served as speaker of the Rhode Island House of Representatives (1907–11) and as lieutenant governor of the state (1913–15).

Pictured here is the Number 1 School, *c.* 1914, at the junction of Warren's Point Road and Sakonnet Point Road. In 1885 there were ten school districts, each having a summer and winter term. The summer term started in April or May, and the winter term in November or December.

The Number 5 School (*c.* 1846), the stone schoolhouse, was located at 209 Long Highway. The town bought this land from Stephen Simmons in 1846 and built the school shortly thereafter. It remained in educational use until 1928. The property was bought by Ambrose Bliss in 1930 and remodeled as a dwelling in the style of a French country cottage.

This photograph is of the Number 9 School (c. 1845), located at 456 Long Highway (south), c. 1907. This building continued in its original function until the completion of the Wilbur School. Schools opened at nine o'clock in the morning and consisted of two, three-hour sessions with a break of one hour allowed.

Adamsville Hill School Number 6 is shown here, c. 1914, at the corner of John Dyer Road. Each scholar was entitled to a 15-minute recess. At the discretion of the teacher, endeavoring to keep order or discipline, he or she could cause a scholar to have recess alone.

Pictured here is the Adeline E.H. Slicer House, or "The Mill," (*c.* mid-19th century), *c.* 1914. It is a striking, shingled house, built in two stages. The original section is a three-story, conical-roof, octagonal-plan gristmill around which wraps a later, one-and-one-half-story section with a sweeping roof, prominent stone chimneys, and inset porches. Mrs. Slicer employed the state's highly regarded architectural firm of Stone, Carpenter, & Willson to design the conversion. The architects employed Sydney Burleigh to execute the interior decorative trim. This property is an exquisite and unusual house, important for its artistic collaboration, for its method of construction, and as one of the town's best "shingle-style" summer homes of the 1880s.

Nine
Down S'cunnet Way

This is the view looking east on West Main Road from the Patten residence, *c.* 1914. This is the country where David Patten first developed his appreciation for homily values and his love for S'cunnet. He expressed that fondness so well in his series of "In Perspective" articles for the *Journal-Bulletin.*

Pictured here is the Dora Wilbour Patten House (*c.* 1908–09), 541 West Main Road. Mrs. Patten (1864–1950) built this Colonial Revival house on land that had long belonged to her family, the Wilbours. This is a fine representative of the first generation of the Colonial Revival genre, built generally between 1890 and 1910.

This is a view of the "prairie" from the Patten house. In reality, the "prairie" is the lush hay fields and pastures rolling down to the salt marshes beyond the S'cunnet Point Road. In summer the marsh grass was harvested as winter food for cattle.

Using the site of Dora Wilbour Patten's house as a pivot point, an almost 360-degree, panoramic perspective develops.

Pictured here is a cottage called "Oneonta." Although many of the summer cottages built in the Vernacular Revival Style appear generally unpretentious and may suggest a lack of concern for design, they are in reality superbly well planned for the style of living intended (low-key and informal).

Here is the Simmons-Manchester-Goodrich House (mid-19th century), *c.* 1907, 106 Sakonnet Point Road. This large and elaborate shingled house in Colonial Revival trim was originally built as a Greek Revival cottage by Valentine Simmons (1802–1825). After Simmons's death, the property passed (in 1898) to his granddaughter, Josephine Manchester, and her husband, Lysander. The Manchesters undertook the major remodeling of the property, enlarging and adding the "Colonial" trim. They sold the house in 1901 to Madeleine Lloyd Goodrich. The house is set among several majestic black walnut trees.

The David Sisson "Stone House" (*c.* 1854) is pictured here at 122 Sakonnet Point Road. The land this house stands on was the site of a British raid during the Revolution. In the early 19th century it was the Rotch Farm. David Sisson (1803–1874) bought the land in 1853 and built the house shortly after. David's son, Henry Tillinghast Sisson (1831–1910), acquired the property in 1857. In the late 1870s, H.T. Sisson planned to use the house and land as a summer resort. This plan never materialized.

The James H. Archbold House (*c.* 1924–25), located at 24 Bay Farm Lane, is the subject of this *c.* 1914 photograph. The house is a large and impressive two-and-one-half-story Colonial Revival clapboard-sided dwelling, with a five-bay facade, pediment entrance porch, and three dormers in a gable roof. Archbold was treasurer of the Standard Oil company of Canada. He built this as a summer home.

Sealands, at Warren's Point, *c.* 1915, is typical of the shingle-style summer cottages built by wealthy New York and Midwest families. One of the first of these, the Alden House (*c.* 1886), at 10 Atlantic Avenue, is built on land divided from the Kempton Farm.

Sealands, at Warren's Point, is again pictured here *c.* 1915. The Kempton Farm property included much of the land at Warren's Point. By covenant, purchasers of lots were guaranteed a right-of-way to Warren's Point Beach.

Here is another view of Sealands. Warren's Point deeds restricted the selling of alcoholic beverages. Such restrictions ensured the creation of a quiet, residential summer colony. By 1915 a number of large shingled houses overlooked the Atlantic Ocean from this spot.

The sustenance garden of Mrs. A.D. Park at Warren's Point is shown here. The informal development of Warren's Point as a summer colony beginning in the late 1880s encouraged the first and largest of Little Compton's speculative real estate schemes—Harry T. Sisson's "Seaconnet Park," which went largely unrealized. Sisson planned a development of organized plots extending east from Sakonnet River to beyond Long Pond and north from the ocean to beyond Sakonnet Point Road.

In the Children's Pageant, little milk maids pay tribute to Little Compton's dairy industry, on September 5, 1914. O.E. Dubois published 15 images of the Little Compton Children's Pageant—of those, five are presented here. In Volume I we erroneously identified the Statue of Liberty tableau on p. 106 as a Fourth of July float. We now have reason to believe the pageant is in commemoration of the 240th anniversary of the founding of Little Compton.

In another part of the Children's Pageant, pilgrims and natives were seen in the wilderness float, on September 5, 1914. By the 1660s, the General Court at Plymouth allowed early settlers as well as "freemen" to covenant with the natives to buy land on the Sakonnet River. The parcel that the proprietors acquired by deed in November of 1673 was an approximately 4.5-square-mile rectangle in the town's northwest corner.

In this picture of the Children's Pageant, on September 5, 1914, pilgrims are going to church. Within the parcel, there were 32 surveyed lots—narrow rectangular strips that ran the full width of the purchase—between the present-day Tiverton town line and Taylor's Lane. These lots, arranged in linear fashion, were oriented north to south. The road (West Main Road) paralleled the shore and ran through the middle of the lots.

This is the Potters School Garden Club float, from the Children's Pageant on September 5, 1914. The petitioners for the Sakonnet lands met in July of 1673 to establish articles of association. The several conditions imposed that required a penalty of forfeiture of property to the company reflect the decreasing availability of unclaimed land.

The Warren's Point group was another part of the Children's Pageant. The Plymouth Court declared the lands at Sakonnet a township in 1674, and on April 10 of that year, the landowners met at Duxbury, paid their dues, and drew lots for the first purchase. Only Benjamin Church is known to have occupied his purchase, but he abandoned it during King Philip's War and later settled in Bristol.

This is the drive to the Watch House. As the eager vacationer approached the grand Watch House Inn, the large summer houses of the wealthy, and the less ostentatious cottages of Providence and Fall River day-trippers, loomed along the oceanfront.

Seen here is the easterly view from the Watch House, c. 1905. Spacious and well-manicured lawns, tennis courts, and a panoramic view of the Atlantic awaited guests at the commodious hotel. (For more on the Watch House see Tiverton and Little Compton, Vol. I, pp. 111–113.)

The westerly view from the Watch House is shown in this image. This *c.* 1905 photograph dramatically emphasizes the lay and cluster of the Sakonnet Point summer colony. The large building near the shore is the Sakonnet Inn, also known as the Lyman.

Lloyd's Beach and the Sakonnet settlement can be seen on the horizon in this *c.* 1910 photograph. Little Compton's summer colony development, which was undertaken by newly arrived investors as well as longtime town residents, was never carried out on a large scale (perhaps as a reaction to the unfortunate failure of Sisson's Seaconnet Park).

This is Landsend, at Warren's Point, *c.* 1915. The earliest of summer homes were commodious, shingled affairs, drawing heavily on the architectural forms of colonial New England. These summer homes from the late 19th and early 20th centuries embodied two themes in American architecture: the colonial and the picturesque.

Pictured here is Anthony Cottage, *c.* 1910. Summer residents made a far more sweeping impact on the town. Like other Rhode Island seaside summer spots (Newport, Jamestown, Watch Hill, and Narragansett), Little Compton's shore drew crowds of land-locked out-of-staters.

Here is modest and academic Eaton Cottage, *c*. 1910. Early summer residents either boarded or rented existing farmhouses, but by the early 1880s, construction of summer houses had begun.

A sweeping view of Sakonnet Harbor is seen in this *c*. 1910 photograph. The Lyman Inn is to the left and steamer dockage is at right.

A curving, sandy beach welcomes sunbathers in this *c.* 1910 photograph. The Warren's Point Beach Club consisted of a modest wood-frame office and shingled bathhouses. The private beach club was established in the early years of this century when sunbathing became a popular family leisure activity. This is an especially charming, candid photograph, and even though the identities of the family of vacationers are unknown, we feel compelled to publish it.

Here is seagrass and surf at the Sakonnet bathing beach, c. 1910. Little Compton families familiar with the serenity and cooling Atlantic breezes, persuaded friends to summer here—thus over the following decades, the area's popularity grew as did its summer population.

"Last one in is a rotten egg." Warren's Point Beach Club is pictured here, c. 1910. The beach club was set between two rocky promontories. We assume the shanties on the upper shore are changing pavilions. These were destroyed in the 1938 hurricane.

Warren's Point takes its name from the point on the south coast first settled in the 17th century by Nathaniel Warren. In the top-center background, the Sakonnet Point Light can be seen.

Surf and sand, and lovely linen-clad Misses are seen here, c. 1910. Readers familiar with Dubois's photographs know that he often employed his daughters as models. These two girls appear in several of Dubois's seaside photographs.

This is a view of the "Point" from the Watch House, *c.* 1912. At the top and left is West Island. From the late 1860s to about the first decade of the 1900s, this remote outpost was a retreat for wealthy, big-city sports-fishermen.

West Island and Sakonnet Point are pictured here. An underwater telephone line connected the island to Little Compton. During Prohibition, rumrunners made the clubhouse a storage and distribution point for illicit liquor taken from large, off-shore mother ships.

Seen here is West Island and its exclusive "Fishing Club," c. 1919. The disastrous hurricane of September 1938 swept away the buildings of West Island. On the Point, the Sakonnet Inn, the Fo'c's'le Restaurant, and the fish markets, dining halls, and provenders that established this seaside place as a village were also devastated. Except for the restaurant and the commercial fishing structures, nothing was rebuilt. Thus this natural disaster ended the Point's long and important role as a seaside resort.

The Shore Road is pictured here. Little Compton's wide-angle views of the Atlantic Ocean, long-admired by summer visitors, also attracted the attention of the United States War Department on the eve of WW II. Warren's Point Road is the site of two reinforced-concrete, 6-inch gun emplacements (see Chapter One, p. 11).

A large summer cottage allows its owner a magnificent, unencumbered ocean view, c. 1917. The first builders on the Point, such as the Alden family at 10 Atlantic Avenue (c. 1886), encouraged their friends and family to join them, and by 1915 a number of large, shingled houses rose up to overlook the Atlantic.

This is the Cove at Sakonnet, *c.* 1910. Pleasure boating became a fashionable pastime among late-19th-century, well-to-do Rhode Islanders. From the earliest days, Sakonnet Cove has played host to an eclectic mix of work and pleasure boats.

This view is in the lee of the Sakonnet Breakwater, *c.* 1950. The Sakonnet Point Yacht Club, established in 1935, plays an important part in the town's recreational life.

The Sakonnet steamer *Queen City* is pictured here, c. 1900. Few traces remain of Little Compton's Sakonnet summer colony. By the end of the 19th century, the Sakonnet Steamboat Company was running daily trips to Providence with the *Queen City* and the *Awashonks*. These excursions were run primarily during the warmer months. The company also owned and operated the shore dinner hall at Sakonnet Point, and in 1887 they built the imposing Sakonnet Inn.

The steamer *Islander* is pictured at her Sakonnet landing, *c.* 1914. Beginning in 1886, Captain Horatio N. Wilcox operated the ferry run between Providence and Sakonnet Point with the steamer *Dolphin*. The *Dolphin* made calls at Bristol Ferry, Stone Bridge, Newtown (Portsmouth), and Fogland. Wilcox's steamer service on the 66-foot *Dolphin* opened the Providence market to farmers in the southeastern part of the state. About one year after Wilcox began his service, Captain Julius A. Pettey and others organized the Sakonnet Steamboat Company. They

initiated their service with the 92-foot *Queen City*. Later, they added the 104-foot *Awashonks*—she ran for several years until destroyed by fire in 1901. *Awashonks* was replaced by the 106-foot steamer *Islander*. By 1915, only the *Islander*, owned by Philip W. Almy, made the Providence-to-Sakonnet run. Almy also owned the dining pavilion at the Point—a round-trip ticket on the ferry entitled the bearer to a shore dinner.

Pictured here is the Sakonnet steamer *Awashonks*, c. 1900. After the 1938 hurricane, other modes of transportation became more attractive to commuters, and the steamers became uneconomical to run. When day trips by sea began to phase out, and the once-romantic steamers no longer stopped at Narragansett Bay ports, an end came to many marine activities, as well as to repair shops, foundries, shipyards, and chandlers. The coal yards slowed down, and it was only a few years before wharves that had always been kept in good repair became inactive and rundown.

The Joseph R. Burroughs [sic] [Burrows] House (1927), located at 7 Montana Road, is seen here. It was a handsome, Craftsman-built, low, one-and-one-half-story, banded-shingle bungalow, with grouped windows, rubblestone chimney, wraparound porch, and broad sweeping gable roof with dormers and exposed rafter ends.

This is the F.H. Shaw Cottage. Summer cottages built in the bungalow-style were popular as informal vacation homes. The Florence Sayles Hough House, next to the Burrows cottage (see above), is similar in its Craftsman-like construction.

The Conners House is pictured here, *c.* 1910. It was a two-and-one-half-story, three-bay, shingled house with wrap-around porch partly enclosed, and a detached, shingled garage. Eventually, it was the bungalow style that finally became the most popular style in East Coast vacation colonies in the early years of the 20th century.

The Sakonnet Inn (1887), also known as Lyman House, is shown in this *c.* 1915 photograph. This large, two-and-one-half-story, shingled inn featured spacious apartments with ocean views. The inn was built by the Sakonnet Steamboat Corporation as an inducement for vacationers to use the corporation's steamers, the *Queen City* and the *Awashonks*.

This is the west seawall, at Sakonnet Point, *c*. 1915. The storms of the past half century have battered this once well-laid buttress to rubble.

Here is a view of Sakonnet Harbor, looking east, *c*. 1915. Recreational and commercial vessels share anchorage in the snug cove of Sakonnet Harbor.

Lake Josephine is pictured here, c. 1905. On Little Compton's south shore are several saltwater, coastal ponds separated from the ocean by barrier beaches. The 225-acre Briggs marsh is historically valuable as a wildlife preserve. The marsh is a place of rest and feed for migratory Canadian geese, which are the source of the name given to this area by the aboriginal peoples who lived here (Sakonnet: "The black goose comes").

This was a foggy morning at Sakonnet Harbor, c. 1905. The only source of the area's natural freshwater is Simmons Pond, fed by Cold Brook, that drains into Quicksand Pond in the northeast part of town. The few brooks in town (Adamsville, Cold, Sisson, and Dundery) are shallow and slow moving.

Here is Sakonnet Point Road, at the intersection of Cove Road, *c.* 1930. A thriving mercantile center huddled around the cove. Here, summer residents and commercial fishermen were supplied with all their needs. None of these businesses were reestablished after the 1938 hurricane.

C.R. Wilbur's Sakonnet Point Store, on the boardwalk, is shown in this *c.* 1915 photograph. At this modest store, Mr. Wilbur sold groceries, ice, and automotive oil. Hardly had the horse been replaced by the automobile and the stable by the garage, when a new enterprise evolved, as witnessed by the sign on the side of the building: "Automobiles for hire."

Pictured here is Main Street at Sakonnet Point, c. 1905. On the rim of the harbor, places like the Davis family house (right) offered room and board to vacationers. Like other seaside towns in southern New England, Sakonnet Point enjoys weather that is relatively moderate—warmed in the winter by the gulf stream and cooled in the summer by sea breezes. These conditions played a major role in developing the area as a summer resort. As an aid to orientation, the reader is advised to scan these Sakonnet Point images for the watertower in the background. Because most of what is illustrated in this chapter was washed away or destroyed by the 1938 hurricane, the reader will be hard-pressed to find any manmade landmarks still existing.

Sakonnet Steamboat Company's pier and the casino, c. 1912. The steamboat company's casino and dance hall were the destination of thousands of seasonal visitors from Providence and Fall River who traveled to Bristol, Portsmouth, or Tiverton to take the pleasant steamboat excursion to Rhode Island's remote resort.

The Sakonnet Dining Hall, 1906. The hurricane of September 21, 1938, swept Sakonnet Point clean of all its buildings: the Sakonnet Inn, the casino and dining hall, the fish markets, the chandlers, and the handsome, Craftsman-built cottages. This catastrophe forever changed the face of the area and removed all evidence of the Point's long and important role as Little Compton's third village.

Here is another view of the Sakonnet Point dining hall, c. 1910. After the devastation wrought by the 1938 hurricane, a conscious decision was made not to rebuild the area as a resort. This suggests that the hey-day of the day-excursion steamer had passed.

Pictured here is the Fo'c's'le Restaurant and Cove Market (c. 1939), c. 1945. It is a sprawling, one-story, vertical-board and shingled building, with many windows on the east side overlooking the harbor. This building is on the same site as the original casino and Bluff Head Fish Market that were washed out to sea during the 1938 hurricane.

Here is the Sakonnet Point fishing fleet, *c.* 1950. Maritime activity has played a varying role in Little Compton's economy. The lack of safe harbor in the 19th century made establishment of a large commercial fleet difficult. The 1850 census records no fishermen living at the Point, and only 17 in 1865, 19 in 1875, and 11 in 1885.

The Sakonnet Point fishing fleet is seen again in this *c.* 1980 photograph. The legacy of fishing activity here is relatively minor. Maritime-related structures date from the mid-20th century. The area just north of Sakonnet Point Harbor is vulnerable and exposed to storms and heavy seas.

United States Volunteer Life Saving Corps members practice shooting the lifeline, *c.* 1905. The authors found no record of a permanent lifesaving station at Sakonnet Point. However, we may safely assume that some sort of organized lifesaving operation had its presence there. In its report of 1906, the Rhode Island chapter of the USVLSC numbered 300 members staffing 60 crews.

Pictured here is a launching of the lifesaving boat, *c.* 1907. As transportation improved, and vacationers flocked to seaside resorts, there came an increase in water-related accidents. The Rhode Island USVLSC patrolled and placed lifesaving equipment at all the dangerous places along Narragansett Bay.

The crew is bringing in the lifeboat in this *c.* 1907 postcard. Because lighthouses were not well equipped with lifesaving apparatus, the USVLSC established lifesaving stations along the shores, close to lighthouses, and in some spots where crowds were largest during the summer months. Bait shops, wharves, ferry landings, canoe clubs, yacht clubs, chandlers, hotels, and beach clubs were all equipped with emergency lifesaving gear by the Corps.

This is the cannon at Sakonnet, *c.* 1905. This massive cannon was on the property of the Macauley house on an outcrop of ledge to the east of Sakonnet Point Road. The exact use of this cannon is unknown, but it is suggested that it is the type used by the Volunteer Lifesaving Corps to fire signals in storms to stranded mariners.

Acknowledgments

The authors are deeply indebted to, and acknowledge, the unselfish generosity of several Tiverton and Little Compton people who loaned precious family photographs.

Foremost, we thank Arthur Waddicor for his enthusiastic search of his photo archives on our behalf. Art lent rare volumes and pamphlets from his personal research library, and personally conducted a tour of Weetamoo Woods. Photographs taken on that tour are included in a special Weetamoo Woods section. Art's knowledge and love of Tiverton history and archaeology helped to make our work much easier.

Again, we offer grateful thanks to Joseph J. Bains of Braintree, Massachusetts, for allowing us to borrow his rare O.E. Dubois photo postcards. Joe is a native Rhode Islander with roots in Bristol and Prudence Island. He is active in historic research and conservation, and he has contributed in a major way to all of our Images publications.

Others deserving of special thanks for loans of photos and anecdotal references to local history include: Florence Archambault, Edwina King, Bernard and Terry Shapiro, Elizabeth Reed, Helene Riley, Thelma Manchester Sanford, Marilyn Dennis, Marjorie Carter Simmons of the Little Compton Congregational Church, Debby Bodington Sullivan, and Debby's mother, Georgie Bodingon. Thanks also to Leanne Medeiros and Barbara Eiserlo, who gave us leads to important sources.

It is so reassuring to know there are still longtime residents of the Pocasset and Sakonnet lands who understand the value of our effort—appreciative that it is a legacy to future holders of this narrow and fragile strip of Rhode Island.

A Personal Note

Thanks to Richard V. Simpson, who generously gave me the opportunity to be published. Also to my children, Darcy and James Jr., for always supporting and encouraging their mother's dreams.

—Nancy J. Devin